The Highlands
of Scotland

including the Isle of Skye

Photography by Colin Baxter

Text by Norman Newton

LOMOND BOOKS
EDINBURGH • SCOTLAND

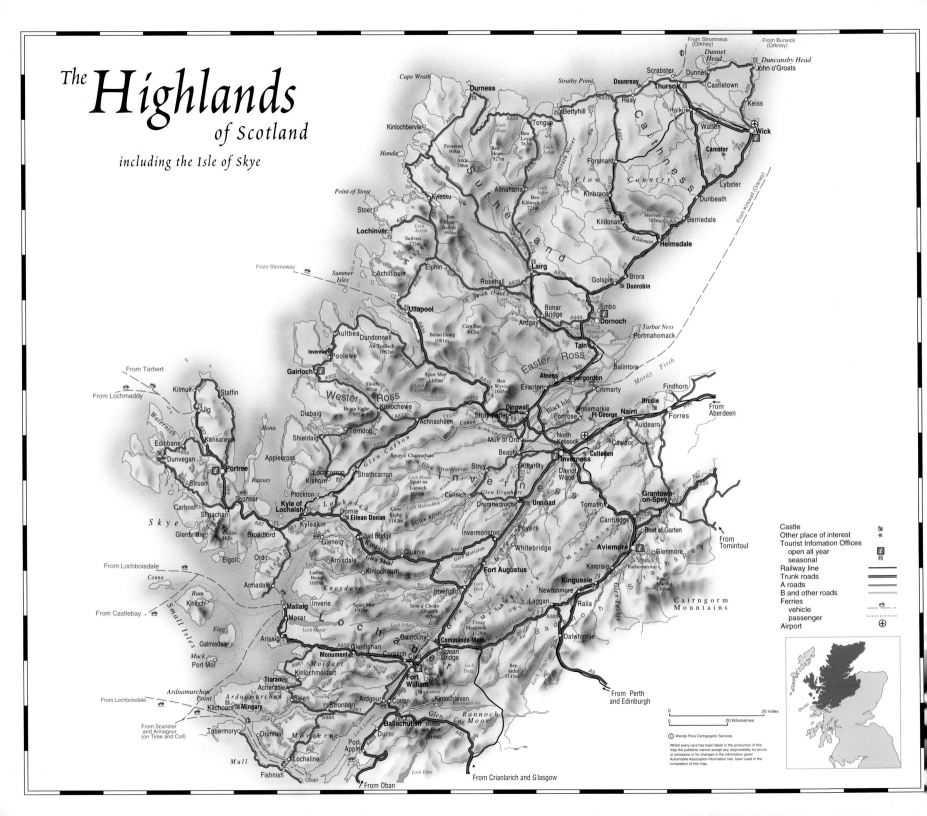

The Highlands
of Scotland
including the Isle of Skye

Castle
Other place of interest
Tourist Infomation Offices
  open all year
  seasonal
Railway line
Trunk roads
A roads
B and other roads
Ferries
  vehicle
  passenger
Airport

0   20 miles
0   20 Kilometres

© Wendy Price Cartographic Services

Whilst every care has been taken in the production of this
map the publisher cannot accept any responsibility for errors
or omissions or for changes in the information given.
Automobile Association information has been used in the
compilation of this map.

The Highlands
of Scotland

including the Isle of Skye

CONTENTS

The Highlands of Scotland

Introduction

The Highlands of Scotland – an area of outstanding natural beauty, and harrowing human history – appeal to a wide range of visitors and have been a destination for tourists and 'excursionists' for over two hundred years. The land of the mountain and the flood, celebrated in verse and song by generations of exiles since the middle of the eighteenth century, it can be almost painfully beautiful or cruelly demanding – sometimes on the same day. The scenery of the Highlands is justifiably famous: there are few parts of the world with such a range of natural beauty, with some of the oldest rocks in the world ranged alongside more recent volcanic landscapes, all subject to the processes of glaciation during the last Ice Age. The present landscape is not always a natural wilderness, but sometimes man-made, whether by the early agriculturalists of the Neolithic period and the Bronze Age, or more recently due to overgrazing by the sheep and cattle which replaced most of the human inhabitants in the nineteenth century.

The history of the Highlands is long and bloody, and there are reminders everywhere in the form of ruined castles and monuments dating from the Viking period and the Middle Ages to the poignant war memorials of the twentieth century. The Highlands have been occupied many times, notably by Norse settlers (AD 800-1150), by Anglo-Norman invaders who settled in the fertile Lowlands and the coastal plains of the Highlands in the eleventh and twelfth centuries, by Cromwellian forces during the civil wars of the seventeenth century, and by troops representing the Government of the United Kingdom of Great Britain and Ireland, after the Jacobite rebellions of 1715 and 1745.

Sometimes the invaders were not military men: in the nineteenth century many Highland lairds (landowners) evicted the local population from their farms and cottages and replaced them with Lowland shepherds, brought into the glens to run the vast flocks of sheep which were far more profitable than people. The process known as 'The Highland Clearances' began in the last years of the eighteenth century, but reached its peak in the middle of the nineteenth century, by when many thousands of Highlanders had emigrated, either by choice or by force, to the new colonies in North America, Australia and New Zealand. Each summer their descendants return, keen to trace their ancestry and find their roots.

Until the late nineteenth century, most Highlanders were Gaelic-speaking, and immersed in Gaelic culture. Today, Gaelic speakers number certainly less than 100,000 out of a Scottish population of over five million. Perhaps only half that number are native speakers, and many of them now live in Scotland's cities. Gaelic is strongest in the Outer Hebrides and on the island of Skye. Only a few hundred native speakers are left on the mainland; many of them reside in Inverness. Despite these statistics, Gaelic is fighting vigorously for survival, and many talented people promote the cause. One of the most obvious signs of

LOCH DÙGHAILL, or 'Dougal's Loch', Sleat Peninsula, Isle of Skye (opposite). Mountains, moors and lochs are typical ingredients of the Highlands of Scotland.

LOCH TORRIDON, WESTER ROSS
Light and colour play an integral part in a powerful mountain landscape.

Gaelic culture is in the place-names of the Highlands, though along the west coast, and in the islands, most of the place-names are Gaelic versions of Norse names, fixed firmly during the 350 years of Norse occupation, starting around AD 800.

In this book, 'The Highlands' means effectively the area presently administered by the Highland Council, extending from Caithness in the north to Ballachulish, Loch Leven and Dalwhinnie in the south, and from Skye and the Small Isles in the west to Nairn and Auldearn in the east. The old counties disappeared in the local government reorganisation of 1975, but the current Highland area includes Caithness, Sutherland, Ross and Cromarty, Inverness-shire and Nairn; excluded are the parts of the Outer Hebrides which were administered by the counties of Ross and Cromarty and Inverness-shire; included are parts of the former county of Argyll now regarded as part of Lochaber – Ardnamurchan and Morvern. The history of local government in the Highlands is complicated, but important to people researching family history, who need to know which parish their ancestors lived in.

Getting around the Highlands and Islands is much easier than it used to be. Fast, modern roads connect all the major centres, and Inverness is linked to the south by the new, improved, realigned and widened A9, the major trunk road through the middle of Scotland. There are airports at Wick and at Dalcross, east of Inverness, with links to Orkney, Shetland, Stornoway, Aberdeen, Glasgow, Edinburgh, all three London airports, and Amsterdam. The island of Skye is now linked to the mainland by a controversial toll bridge, and also by two car ferries, from Mallaig to Armadale and from Glenelg to Kylerhea (summer only).

However, there are still many miles of single-track roads in the Highlands, and some advice to the traveller will avoid problems. Passing places are provided at frequent intervals, and motorists are urged to use these courteously, to allow oncoming traffic to pass, and to allow following traffic to overtake.

A few more pieces of practical advice: if hill-walking, dress for all weathers, and wear stout footwear. Wellies are positively dangerous in wet conditions on the hills and should be reserved for wading. Most Scots regard access to the hills as a birthright, but foreign landowners do not always agree, so it pays to take local advice. In the shooting season, it is only common sense to enquire locally to see if there are any shooters in the hills. And then, there are the midges! They are a menace, and unrelenting. Various commercial potions claim to repel them, but on a midgey day the best thing is to avoid them, by staying away from damp, dark, sheltered areas. When the midges are at their worst, the best place for a picnic is on the most windswept site you can find, preferably in the sunshine, which is not as rare in the West Highlands as some would have you believe.

The natural history of the Highlands can never be taken for granted. The flora and fauna which inhabit our scenic landscapes are rich, diverse, unusual and often rare. In August the hills burst into colour, as the purple heather blossoms, but throughout the year there are natural pleasures to enjoy. In spring, wildflowers turn the coastal machair into a tapestry of colour, while the yellow of gorse and broom can be seen any month of the year.

One of the distinguishing features of the Highlands is the tremendous range of habitats and ecosystems in a comparatively small area. In only a few miles, habitats can vary from sheltered, lush coastal pockets through sloping hillsides of birch, oak and hazel, to peat bogs and moorland, and finally to alpine species. Small wonder the area is so popular with botanists, from specialists in mosses and lichens to the conservators of the ancient Caledonian pine forest.

With such diversity of habitats, it is no surprise that the range of bird and animal life is equally broad. Visitors are amazed to see how prolific Highland bird life is: the crossbill and capercaillie, superbly adapted to life in the pine forest, grouse, denizen of the higher

LOCH KANAIRD, WESTER ROSS Midsummer sunset, north of Ullapool. The landscape here assumes a wild and beautiful guise.

THE KINTAIL MOUNTAINS & LOCH DUICH
Looking east from above Loch Duich towards Kintail, one of the grandest mountain ranges west of the Great Glen.

grounds, the ospreys of Strathspey and of course the golden eagles which soar above the highest mountains and craggiest terrain.

The animals of the Highlands are not as prolific as they once were – the brown bear disappeared by the tenth century AD, while in later centuries the beaver, wild boar and wolf were hunted to extinction. But foxes, pine martens, badgers and red deer survive in large numbers, while around the coasts, otters and two species of seals are thriving.

Finally, respect both the people and the landscape of the Highlands. You will find hospitality and friendliness unmatched anywhere else in the British Isles. This book gives you some ideas, in words and pictures, where to go in the Highlands for the best scenery and the most interesting history, but the best way to explore the Highlands is to equip yourself with plenty of time, and prepare to wander.

Inverness

The town of Inverness is the 'Hub of the Highlands', the administrative capital of the region and centre of its transport network. Linked to Glasgow, Edinburgh and London by both rail and air services, and with road connections in all directions, most visitors to the Highlands will pass through Inverness at some stage.

Inverness in the 1950s was a small Scottish provincial town with a population of 28,000, but in the last 50 years it has grown to the point where the population now exceeds 50,000. New housing estates have spread up the lower slopes of the prehistoric hill fort of Craig Phadraig to the west, but most of the expansion has been to the east, where the tiny villages of Balloch, Smithton, Culloden and Cradlehall have been transformed into suburbs.

Inverness is a busy, modern town, with a full range of services and facilities for both residents and visitors. Sadly, the historic heart of the town was swept away in the 1960s in the name of progress, much to the regret of native Invernessians. Almost nothing remains of medieval Inverness, apart from a couple of buildings on Church Street. The Town House, an example of late-Victorian architectural extravagance, is the most impressive building remaining. Beside it is Inverness Museum, where the archaeology and natural history of the area are displayed and explained. There is an important collection of Jacobite material, and a small art gallery. The Tourist Information Centre is located on the ground floor of the Museum building.

Amongst the many other features of the Inverness area are the Aquadome and Sports Centre in the Bught Park, with swimming and leisure facilities; Balnain House, the 'Home of Highland Music', where the history of the classical music of Gaelic culture,

*INVERNESS
The River Ness
winds its way through
the centre of the
'Capital of the
Highlands'.*

*INVERNESS
CASTLE,
overlooking the
River Ness, was built
in the nineteenth
century as a prison
and court-house,
replacing an earlier
medieval fortress.*

pibroch bagpipe music, is explained; and Inverness
Public Library, with an excellent collection of books
on Highland history and culture. Much of the history
of the Highlands is contained in local newspapers
which are available for consultation in the Library, on
microfilm, with indexes by both subjects and personal
names for the period 1809-1900.

For those interested in researching their family tree,
Highland Archives has Census records on microfilm
for all Highland parishes, every ten years from 1841 to
1891, and also Old Parish Registers of births, baptisms,
marriages and deaths, as well as the International
Genealogical Index compiled by the Mormon church.
Highland Archives employs a full-time genealogist, and
is located in the same building as the Public Library, at
Farraline Park. Eden Court Theatre is almost certainly

one of the most important cultural facilities in the
Highlands and enjoys widespread support from the
scattered population.

There has been a settlement at the point at which
the River Ness flows into the Beauly Firth since
prehistoric times, but the first time the area enters the
historic record is in the 580s, when St Columba of
Iona passed through and had his encounter with
Nessie, the Loch Ness Monster, preserved for posterity
by his biographer, Adomnan. It is the first eye-witness
account of Nessie, and is interesting in that the
episode took place not in Loch Ness, where Nessie
now resides, but in the River Ness.

Situated at the northern end of the Great Glen, that
geological gash splitting the Highlands in two,
Inverness is ideally suited to be the capital of the
Highlands. It has a long history as a Royal Burgh,
though in the Middle Ages it competed with other
towns for the position of supremacy it has achieved
today. Strategically, Inverness was the key to
maintaining control of the Highlands, and the north of
Scotland, and over the centuries has been taken and
retaken numerous times by competing forces.

On two notable occasions Inverness found itself
involved in conflicts which affected the course of
Scottish history. In 1411 Donald of the Isles, Lord of
the Isles and Earl of Ross, arrived at the town at the
head of a massive army of Highlanders and Islanders.
They burnt the famous bridge and sacked the town.
The burghers of Inverness offered little resistance,
though one man, John Cumming, put on his armour
and head-piece, took up his two-handed sword, and
stood at the end of the town bridge to defy the might

of the MacDonald and his armies. It was said that had there been ten men as brave as John Cumming in Inverness, neither the bridge nor the town would have been destroyed.

Donald of the Isles went on to fight one of the great set-piece battles of Scottish history. His failure to win decisively at the Battle of Harlaw, where his Highland army met the force of the Scottish Crown near Aberdeen, ensured that the dominance of the Scottish state, and the decline of Gaelic-speaking chieftains, would inevitably place Highland culture and Highland people under continuous and increasing pressure.

These historical processes reached their seemingly inevitable conclusion on 16 April 1746 on Drumossie Muir, just outside Inverness. The Battle of Culloden ended Bonnie Prince Charlie's Jacobite rebellion of 1745-6. Although the battle was fought just up the hill from Culloden House, on what is now called Culloden Moor, this was a battle for the control of Inverness. The carnage on the day was dreadful; the cruelty of the successful Government troops afterwards was terrible, even by the standards of the time.

The northern end of the Caledonian Canal reaches the sea at Inverness, in a series of locks. Begun in 1803 by Thomas Telford, it took 20 years to complete and was one of the great engineering feats of the nineteenth century. It links the North Sea with the Atlantic Ocean, but never fulfilled the economic promise anticipated by its planners. Its importance was minimised by the coming of the railways in the last half of the nineteenth century. Today it is used mainly by leisure craft, but is still an important route for some fishing boats.

INVERNESS FROM THE AIR
Road and foot bridges link the two sides of the town. The Kessock Bridge in the distance spans the Moray Firth to the Black Isle.

Around Loch Ness

One of the most interesting day excursions in the Highlands is the circuit of Loch Ness, best attempted in a clockwise direction. Driving south from Inverness, heading for the little village of Dores at the northern end of Loch Ness, thoughts inevitably turn to the possibilities of sighting Nessie, the Loch Ness Monster. The term was first coined in 1933 in the columns of the *Inverness Courier*, but was quickly adopted worldwide. There is a wide spectrum of belief about Nessie, with many true believers and a diminishing hard core of sceptics. What cannot be denied, is that many hundreds of eye-witnesses are convinced that they have seen something. What is not so easy, is to explain what they have seen. There are many possible explanations for sightings, ranging from half-submerged logs to various life forms, including deer, otters, seals, sturgeon, and giant eels. Unfortunately various hoaxes, including fake footprints and the famous picture of Nessie, the 'Surgeon's photograph', recently exposed as a fraud, do nothing to encourage belief in the existence of a previously unidentified species. Nessie has been hunted by the latest electronic technology, by a professional Nessie-hunter, by a miniature submarine, and by an unending stream of eccentrics.

The road down the east side of Loch Ness was part of the network built by General Wade, and his successor Major Caulfeild, in the years following the 1715 Jacobite rebellion, as part of the military occupation of the Highlands. The road along the west side of the loch, now part of the main road from Fort William to Inverness, was not completed until the 1930s – when the Nessie sightings started. After Dores, the line of the old Wade road gives a good view of the loch.

Approaching Foyers, on the eastern side, Boleskine House is a typical example of an eighteenth-century tacksman's house, but is unfortunately better known today for its brief association with Aleister Crowley, professional eccentric and practitioner of black magic, who used it for house parties up to the 1920s; its reputation has not been enhanced by the succession of celebrities who have owned it since.

Only a few hundred people live on Loch Ness-side, despite its proximity to Inverness, but at one time it was a must for every tourist visiting Scotland. The main attraction was the Falls of Foyers. Boswell and Johnson visited it in the 1770s, and wrote about it, which enhanced its image. Burns and Southey were both impressed. The Upper Falls consist of three leaps, and the Lower Falls, which are more impressive, cascade into an amphitheatre of rock after a fall of about 90 ft (30 m).

This is not a part of Scotland usually associated with industrial archaeology, but Foyers is famous in industrial history as the site of Scotland's first commercial hydro-electric scheme, opened in 1908 to provide power for an aluminium smelter which did not finally close until 1967. A modern power station continues to render the Falls less impressive than the obviously dramatic natural phenomenon which made such an impact on early tourists.

South of Foyers the road diverges from Loch Ness, through an area of attractive moorland and wooded

URQUHART CASTLE AND LOCH NESS (opposite). The existing ruins of the tower and walls date from the seventeenth century, though the castle is probably built on the site of an ancient Pictish fort.

LOCH NESS FROM THE AIR, looking to the south-east. The loch is some 23 miles (37 km) long and 800 ft (244 m) deep. Its waters run along the geological fault known as 'The Great Glen' and form part of the Caledonian Canal.

hills. From this area, the 'normal' upland landscape of the mountains and glens of the Highlands is suddenly and abruptly intersected by the great geological Rift Valley of Glen Albyn, the Great Glen of Scotland.

At the south end of Loch Ness is the village of Fort Augustus, owing its existence to the military occupation of the Highlands after the Jacobite Rising of 1715. The original barracks were replaced by a fort, built by General Wade in 1730 and not finally sold off until 1867, when a Benedictine order bought the site and incorporated it into a school and abbey. The school is now closed, but, moving with the times, the monks have opened a heritage centre which is proving popular. The locks of the Caledonian Canal in Fort Augustus are an attractive place at which to pause and watch the yachting world go by. There is a seasonal Tourist Information Centre in the village.

In one of those ironies which haunt Highland history, Fort Augustus was named after William

Augustus, Duke of Cumberland, then a nine-year-old boy. Just 16 years later he commanded the Government troops at Culloden on behalf of his father, King George II, and in the aftermath of that battle he used the fort as a base from which to hunt down Jacobite fugitives. The original name of the settlement which Wade made the hub of his road network in this part of the Highlands was Kilchumein, named after St Chumein. The local secondary school preserves this name in Kilchuimen Academy.

South of Fort Augustus is Loch Oich, and the village of Invergarry, where a monument at the 'Well of the Heads' commemorates one of the more gruesome episodes of Highland history. The bloody heads of seven brothers were washed in this well in 1665, so that the chieftain of the MacDonalds of Keppoch could identify the killers of his two sons. The monument was erected in 1812 and has inscriptions in English, French, Latin and Gaelic.

North of Fort Augustus the road between Fort William and Inverness passes through the village of Invermoriston, from where a side road heads up Glenmoriston and over the watershed to Glen Shiel, Loch Duich, Kyle of Lochalsh and the Isle of Skye.

Between Invermoriston and Drumnadrochit a cairn commemorates John Cobb, who was killed in 1952 while pursuing the world water speed record in his speedboat. He was well regarded by many local people because he respected the Sabbath during the weeks of preparation for his fatal attempt.

Just before Drumnadrochit is Urquhart Castle, one of the most important historic sites in the Highlands, as well as one of the most unpronounceable (roughly, 'urr-cart'). The walls date mainly from 1691, when they were blown up to prevent their occupation by Jacobites, but underneath them are the remains of a Dark Age fortress, possibly visited by St Columba in the 580s during his foray into the land of the Picts. Some argue it has a better claim than Craig Phadraig at Inverness as the fort of King Brude of the Picts. The seventeenth-century tower overlooks Urquhart Bay,

one of the most popular haunts of the Loch Ness Monster. The Nessie phenomenon can be studied in the exhibitions in the village of Drumnadrochit.

The main road north from Drumnadrochit leads directly to Inverness, but it is worth exploring some of the alternatives, for example via Cannich and Strathglass, or over the hill to Kiltarlity and Beauly. Part of the enchantment of visiting the Highlands is exploring off the beaten track, and the thrill of discovery of all the out-of-the-way places which are not described in guidebooks and tourist literature.

LOCH AFFRIC
Remnants of the ancient Caledonian pine forest, which once covered much of Scotland, survive down the length of Glen Affric.

Nairn, Badenoch & Strathspey

CAWDOR CASTLE, near Nairn, is associated with Shakespeare's Macbeth.

To the east of Inverness is the old county of Nairn, with its county town of the same name. Nairn suffers from the proximity of Inverness, only 16 miles (25.7 km) away, which has grown in size and economic prosperity as Nairn has remained more sedate, but it is an important and ancient medieval royal burgh. It benefits from a micro-climate which has made it a favourite holiday destination since the growth of tourism in late-Victorian Britain. The arrival of the railway in 1855 opened up the area, and by 1890 it was known as 'The Brighton of the North'. The sands at Nairn are still magnificent, and there are two outstanding links golf courses. The fishertown part of Nairn survives, and there is a little museum in a cottage there preserving mementoes of a way of life rapidly dying out.

Within easy driving distance are several important historic sites which are worth a visit. Cawdor Castle dates from 1454, and is open to the public. The present tower replaced an earlier castle, associated with Macbeth who, as all students of Shakespeare will know, was Thane of Cawdor. There is an interesting legend connected with a hawthorn or yew tree on the site, the remains of which are preserved in the basement. When the Thane needed to build a new castle, he was instructed in a dream to load a chest of gold on to the back of a donkey, turn it loose, and build his new castle on the spot where the beast finally lay down to rest.

The estate passed to the Campbells of Argyll in 1510, and has belonged to the Campbells of Cawdor (more correctly, Calder) ever since. The family were the lairds of the Hebridean island of Islay from 1614 until 1726 and were renowned for being at the forefront of agricultural improvement and innovation.

Culloden battlefield and visitor centre can be reached easily by driving west from Nairn, avoiding the busy traffic of Inverness. The 1746 battle was fought for the control of Inverness, which had been occupied by the Jacobite army for many months. The politics of this period are complicated, and far from the black and white Scotland versus England caricature sometimes presented. More Highlanders signed up to support the cause of the Hanoverian Government than ever supported the obviously doomed adventure of Prince Charles Edward Stuart, son of the Pretender (or claimant) to the British throne. The thousands of Highlanders who enrolled in the 'Independent Companies' were kept well away from the battle at Culloden, but provided the security which allowed the British army to concentrate the full force of its resources on the Jacobite army.

The support of Lowlanders, or Scots from outside the areas dominated by Highland clans, provided more recruits for Bonnie Prince Charlie's armies than the Highland areas where support for the Jacobite cause might have been expected. At Culloden, however, almost all the Scots fighting on the Jacobite side were from Highland clans. Many clan chiefs, though sympathetic to the Stewart cause, saw the futility of resistance and kept out of the conflict altogether. Others openly supported the Government side. Many

of the officers in the Government artillery regiments were Scots. Just to complicate things further, hundreds of French and Irish troops fought for the Jacobite cause.

Culloden was the culmination of a Scottish civil war. Seen from a European perspective, it was a minor episode in a wider power struggle involving the great dynasties of Europe's royal families. However, there was nothing minor about its effect on Highland history and culture – it casts a long shadow.

The battlefield is owned by the National Trust for Scotland: the lines of the opposing armies are laid out, and their standards flutter in the breeze. A large memorial cairn dominates the area where thousands died. A visitor centre on the edge of the battlefield has an interpretive display both of the events of April 1746 and the whole history of the Jacobite cause. There is an excellent bookshop, and a restaurant.

FORT GEORGE FROM THE AIR
The geometric military fortifications were built in the eighteenth century. Modern barracks were added later within the structure.

LOCH AN EILEIN, ROTHIEMURCHUS AND THE CAIRNGORM MOUNTAINS, a majestic landscape and National Nature Reserve.

Near the Culloden battlefield, just down the hill in Strathnairn, are two monumental constructions which are well worth a look. The more ancient of the two sites are the cairns of Clava, dating from the Bronze Age, perhaps from 1500-2000 BC. These are ring-cairns, burial cairns built with great effort and with great accuracy – the entrance passages of two of the three cairns point to the midwinter sunset. Nearby is the viaduct, built in 1893 to carry the Highland Railway over the river Nairn.

On the other side of the battlefield, towards the Moray Firth, lies Culloden House, now a hotel, but once the home of Duncan Forbes of Culloden and his descendants. He rose to become the senior law officer in Scotland before the Jacobite rebellion of 1745, and was unwavering in his support for the Government. Indeed, it was in no small measure due to his efforts that many clan chiefs stayed out of the rising, or even supported the Government cause. He was horrified at the treatment of captured Jacobites and civilians by Cumberland's troops after the battle, and for this reason was not welcome at court, and was never recompensed for the considerable amount of his personal fortune which he invested in ensuring the defeat of the Jacobite cause. It is ironic that the name of Culloden, which through the name

of Duncan Forbes became a byword for support of the Establishment, became, after the battle only a mile up the hill from his house, a name associated with rebellion and with the destruction of the Highland way of life. Bonnie Prince Charlie rather cheekily and pointedly stayed in Culloden House the night before the battle, though not in the current house, which was rebuilt in the 1780s on the foundations of the original structure, destroyed in a fire.

Also to the west of Nairn is the important eighteenth-century fortress of Fort George, another visible reminder of the military occupation of the

CARRBRIDGE
One of General Wade's bridges carrying the military road from Inverness to Perth over the River Dulnain in the village of Carrbridge.

19

THE RIVER SPEY runs along the western flanks of the Cairngorms, through a fertile flood plain, until it reaches the sea at Spey Bay on the Moray Firth.

used in anger. It is still used as an army garrison and training centre. There is a small museum. Nearby is Ardersier, an old fishing village where many of the traditional houses and cottages have been renovated and restored by Inverness commuters.

Brodie Castle, near Forres, is another ancient castle easily visited from Nairn. It is National Trust for Scotland property, and is open to the public. The Brodie family has had a fortification on the site since the twelfth century. It has been rebuilt and added to at various times, but the core of the castle is a Z-plan tower house of the late sixteenth century. Kilravock Castle (pronounced 'Kilrock'), only 2 miles (3.2 km) from Cawdor Castle, is the

Highlands. It was built in 1747-70 as a response to the Jacobite uprising of 1745-6 which ended at Culloden, and was visited by Johnson and Boswell just three years after completion. It takes its name from the Hanoverian monarchs who occupied the British throne during its construction. Fort George is built on a spit of land jutting out into the Moray Firth, matched on the opposite shore by Chanonry Point on the Black Isle, near Fortrose and Rosemarkie, and so is guarding a point of strategic importance. It is one of the best-preserved eighteenth-century fortresses in Europe, and is in pristine condition, never having been

ancestral home of another great Highland family, the Roses (and Rosses). The tower dates from 1460, when the Lords of the Isles, who were also the Earls of Ross at the time, authorised its construction.

The proliferation of ancient estates and important families in this area reflects the fertility and prosperity of the coastlands of the Moray Firth. Inland, the terrain rises gradually to moorland, dissected by river valleys, of which the most important are the Nairn and the Spey. Strathspey is one of the great river valleys of Scotland, and seems to have reclaimed its ancient name after an attempt by the tourist authorities to introduce the concept of the 'Spey Valley'.

The mouth of the Spey, and the ancient burgh of Elgin, are outside the area of the Highlands, but the town of Grantown-on-Spey, once in the county of Moray, moved to Highland Region in 1975 and is now officially part of the Highlands. Another powerful northern family, the Grants, were immodestly responsible for this eighteenth-century planned village, but it failed to become the economic and manufacturing centre envisaged, and survived quietly until in the late nineteenth century it was transformed into a fashion-able health and tourist

resort. The arrival of the railway in 1863 opened up new possibilities for this attractive town, which remains an unspoiled destination for visitors today. Grantown-on-Spey offers a full range of services to the traveller, though trains no longer stop there. Nearby is the village of Carrbridge, with its Landmark Visitor Centre interpreting Highland history and natural history. This area is attractive to people interested in less energetic pursuits, for there are many attractive forest walks and the prospect of seeing

ospreys and other wildlife in local lochs.

Aviemore is the economic powerhouse of the area known as Badenoch and Strathspey. Until the 1960s it was little more than a railway halt on the Highland Railway, but it was selected for development as the first purpose-built tourist town in the Highlands. Today the architecture seems perhaps inappropriate, but locally many people are working hard to rejuv-enate the facilities and to incorporate developments more sympathetically into the surrounding landscape.

THE CAIRNGORM PLATEAU and its northern corries in winter sun. The ski development of Coire Cas is just visible in the foreground.

From Aviemore a short stretch of railway runs to Boat of Garten, part of the pre-Beeching system lovingly recreated by local enthusiasts, using steam engines. There are plans to extend the track further. The station, trains and rolling stock are evocative of a bygone age, and are popular with visitors.

East of Aviemore an access road leads to Glenmore Lodge, an outdoor centre, the Glen More Forest Park and the ski slopes of Cairngorm, where the flora and fauna of the sub-arctic Cairngorm plateau intersect with the demands of mass ski tourism. Although there are records of skiing in the Scottish hills as far back as the 1890s, it was not until the 1960s, and the provision of facilities, that this form of recreation really flourished in the Cairngorms.

To the south of the road to Glenmore Lodge is the Rothiemurchus Forest, where travellers recorded great fir woods as early as the seventeenth century. The place-name in Gaelic is *Rath Mhor Ghiuthais*, 'the plain of the big firs'. The 'big firs' are Scots pine, and nowhere can these spectacular trees be seen in such numbers, or in such density. There are many opportunities in the area for delightful forest walks.

Further up-country, the villages of Kingussie, Newtonmore and Dalwhinnie all have interesting features. The main artery of the A9, the road connecting Inverness to Perth and the Lowlands through the Drumochter Pass, is occasionally closed in the worst winter weather, but for most of the year functions as the principal route to and from the Highlands. Near Kingussie, the Highland Wildlife Park at Kincraig gives a good idea of some of the native flora and fauna of the area, while the Highland Folk Museum (*Am Fasgadh*) founded by Dr Isobel F Grant in 1956 and now run by Highland Council, tells the story of the human natives of Badenoch and of the Highlands generally, with authentic restorations of eighteenth- and nineteenth-century domestic and agricultural life. The main family in these parts were the Comyn lairds, who had a castle where Ruthven Barracks now stands – another survival of the military occupation of the Highlands in the eighteenth century, built following the 1715 rising.

Newtonmore is in Macpherson country, and there is a small Clan Macpherson museum in the village, which lies at the junction of the main A9 road and a road connecting westwards to Spean Bridge and Fort William. Cluny Castle, near Laggan, was the home of the Macphersons of Cluny. Both Kingussie and Newtonmore are renowned for their shinty teams. This sport, played with a stick (the caman) and a ball,

THE GREAT WOOD OF CALEDON
Scotland's native pine forest now survives in only scattered fragments amounting to about one per cent of its original range.

is a very ancient game, and the teams from these two neighbouring villages are usually to be found competing at the end of every season for various cups and trophies. *Camanachd*, to give shinty its Gaelic name, was certainly played in Ireland in 563, when Columba left to come to Iona partly as a result of a quarrel which escalated from a dispute arising during a game of shinty. As now played in Scotland, under the jurisdiction of the Camanachd Association, it has much in common with the Irish game of hurling, and since 1993 the two associations have played international matches. Throughout the Highlands, a game of shinty was part of the way of observing the New Year, and there are many examples of exactly the kind of outbreaks of violence and public disorder arising, no doubt fuelled by liquid celebrations, which resulted in Columba's exile.

The distillation of the amber nectar known as *uisgebeatha* in Gaelic, or as whisky in English, has been an important industry in Badenoch and Strathspey for many centuries. There is a Visitor Centre at the Tomatin Distillery, between Inverness and Grantown-on-Spey, where the processes of distilling can be viewed, and the results sampled. Another example of a working distillery can be seen at Dalwhinnie, the last village on the A9, travelling south, before the Pass of Drumochter. A road from Dalwhinnie to Laggan connects with the road linking Newtonmore to Fort William. This is a wild, windswept area, with severe winter weather, but these isolated villages and settlements, now bypassed by the upgraded A9 trunk road, are worth visiting and exploring.

LOCH LAGGAN BADENOCH, lies alongside the important cross-country route from Newtonmore to Spean Bridge. The National Nature Reserve of Creag Meagaidh stretches north from its shores to a height of 3609 ft (1100 m).

Ardgour, Morvern & Ardnamurchan

GATEWAY TO ARDGOUR, MORVERN AND ARDNAMURCHAN
The short ferry crossing to and from Corran on Loch Linnhe saves a long detour around the head of the loch.

Across Loch Linnhe from the hustle and bustle of Fort William is some of the wildest, most beautiful and most remote landscape in the West Highlands, and some of the last wilderness areas of Europe: Ardgour, Morvern, and the long, west-pointing finger of the Ardnamurchan peninsula. These areas are best reached by the short ferry crossing of Loch Linnhe at the Corran Narrows, 15 miles (24 km) south of Fort William, where a vehicular ferry plies back and forth from early in the morning until late at night.

Passing through Ardgour and Morvern, spare a thought for the population – the ones who are no longer there. These areas were devastated in the clearances and emigrations of the nineteenth century, replaced by landowners with more profitable sheep. The marvellously stark wilderness is not natural, but a result of over-grazing, a permanent reminder of the combination of economic transformation and human tragedy which created the Highland landscape of the twentieth century. Here and there are pockets of 'natural' landscape: in inaccessible gulleys and ravines, on islands and islets too small to be worth grazing, and in precious areas of protected woodland.

One of the most poignant accounts of the nineteenth century is to be found in Rev. Norman Macleod's *Reminiscences of a Highland Parish* (1871). One of a dynasty of Macleod divines, Norman Macleod wrote sympathetically from his Morvern manse of the way of life of a people he had grown up with. He records how, as an old woman living in overcrowded housing conditions in Glasgow, Mary Cameron spoke with great emotion and with a clear memory of the day in 1824 when her family was evicted from the township of Unnimore, in Morvern. She spoke, in Gaelic, of how her husband James carried his mother on his back up the winding trail leading over the hill from Unnimore to the manse near Lochaline. At the top of the hill they paused for a last look back at their modest home, today a

roofless ruin. Mary Cameron remembered the pain of that day, and her husband's words: 'We are not afraid. The world is wide, and God will sustain us'.

From Lochaline there is a car ferry to Mull, from where, after a short drive to Craignure, it is possible to connect with a ferry to Oban, the hub of ferry services to the islands. Passing the manse of Fiunary, where Norman Macleod and his dynasty served the parish of Morvern, the road reaches Drimnin, a Maclean estate. In the north-west corner of Morvern, past Drimnin, and inaccessible by car, is the extensive

village of Auliston, now completely deserted but once home to hundreds of Highlanders. There are many more settlements just like it, scattered throughout the whole length and breadth of the Highlands.

An alternative route from the Corran Ferry leads on to Strontian, a village which has left its mark in the periodic table of elements – strontium, a deadly by-product of nuclear testing in the 1950s and 1960s, was first identified in the lead mines here. Strontian (the accent is on the second syllable) is at the head of Loch Sunart, a particularly beautiful sea loch which penetrates

LOCH MOIDART
is a sea loch which cuts deeply into the district of Moidart, from where many Highlanders emigrated to Cape Breton, Nova Scotia, in the early nineteenth century.

LOCH SUNART, looking towards Beinn Resipol. There are rich broad-leaved woodland reserves on the shores of the loch containing oak, ash, birch, hazel, alder and rowan.

his abandoned wife Amy here, and married a second time to Margaret, daughter of the Stewart who became Robert II, King of Scotland.

The Clanranald branch of Clan Donald descends from Amy, and is thus the senior branch of the extensive MacDonald clan. Castle Tioram was occupied and besieged on several occasions but was finally destroyed during the 1715 rising by Allan MacDonald of Clanranald to avoid its occupation by the Campbells while he was away supporting the Jacobite cause.

To the west of Salen the road winds along the southern coast of the peninsula of Ardnamurchan, through the village of Kilchoan, ending up at the lighthouse at the Point of Ardnamurchan, the most westerly tip of the mainland of Scotland. There is a summer ferry service from Kilchoan to Tobermory, on Mull.

Near Kilchoan is Mingary Castle, one of the ancient fortresses of the Lords of the Isles. James IV held court there in 1495 and took the submission of the island chiefs, during his tour of the west coasts and island. This was designed to stamp royal authority on an area which had been ruled since the 1150s by the

far into the enclosing lands of Morvern and Sunart.

Further to the west, at Salen, the road divides: to the north it winds through the coastal fringes of Moidart to Acharacle, Loch Moidart and Loch Ailort, joining the Fort William-Mallaig road at Kinlochailort; north of Acharacle a side road leads to Castle Tioram (pronounced 'Cheerum'), an important stronghold of the MacDonald Lords of the Isles, probably built in the thirteenth century. It is situated on a rocky islet in Loch Moidart and can be reached on foot at low tide. John, Lord of the Isles in the fourteenth century, left

MacDonald Lords of the Isles, descendants of Somerled, who liberated the islands from Norse rule. Mingary was held for them by the MacIans of Ardnamurchan, one of the most powerful branches of Clan Donald. It became a Campbell stronghold in the 1620s but in 1644 was captured for Montrose by Alasdair 'Colkitto' MacDonald (*Coll Ciotach*, 'left-handed Coll'), then recaptured by General Leslie and restored to the Campbells. It was garrisoned during the Jacobite risings and is now in ruins. The enclosure wall probably dates from the thirteenth century.

Few people, and a few more sheep, live in Ardnamurchan, and it is a wild and unforgiving place, except for a few fertile pockets of good land. A geological map of the peninsula reveals that the western end of the peninsula is in fact an extinct volcano, from which igneous dykes radiate out across the landscape in all directions, like the cracks in a pane of glass through which a bullet has passed. But 65 million years have removed all traces, except to the trained eye, of the cataclysmic events which show up so well and so colourfully on the geologist's maps.

The views from Ardnamurchan Point northwards towards the islands of Muck, Eigg and Rum, and westwards to the islands of Coll and Tiree, make the journey along this long and sometimes difficult road well worthwhile. There is no way to hurry on a single-track road, so allow plenty of time for journeys in these remote places. The distances in miles may seem manageable, but travellers have to adjust to unfamiliar conditions.

West from Fort William is 'The Road to the Isles', passing through Glenfinnan and the districts of Moidart and Morar to the end of the road at the fishing port and railhead of Mallaig. This is the part of Scotland where Bonnie Prince Charlie landed in 1745: his standard was raised at Glenfinnan on 19 August. There, a Monument and a National Trust for Scotland visitor centre commemorate the optimistic beginning of a rebellion which ended disastrously at Culloden in April 1746 – a personal tragedy for Charles Edward Stuart and a social milestone for the people of the Highlands.

The Glenfinnan Monument stands at the head of Loch Shiel, and was erected in 1815 by Macdonald of Glenaladale, a grandson of one of the Prince's original supporters. The Raising of the Standard is remembered each year at an anniversary service. The Monument commemorates not Bonnie Prince

STRONTIAN POST OFFICE near the head of Loch Sunart, on the road to Ardnamurchan.

GLENFINNAN VIADUCT carries the West Highland Line from Fort William to Mallaig.

LOCH SHIEL (opposite). It was at the head of this long loch that Bonnie Prince Charlie raised his standard in 1745.

Charlie but the Highlanders who followed him. For many years it was known that it was leaning slightly, but in more recent times the amount that this 'leaning tower of Glenfinnan' deviates from the vertical has been increasing, and remedial work may be required.

Inland from the NTS centre at Glenfinnan is a magnificent railway viaduct, carrying the main line from Fort William to Mallaig. In the summer months, steam trains operate over this line on some services.

Further west is Loch nan Uamh, an inlet of the Sound of Arisaig, where Bonnie Prince Charlie landed from a French frigate on 5 August 1745, and also

from where he left Scotland for the last time on 20 September 1746, after an exciting six months on the run after the battle of Culloden. The white sands of Arisaig are justly famous, and from several points along this stretch of the 'Road to the Isles' there are wonderful views to the islands of Eigg and Rum, and also northwards to the distant jagged outline of the Cuillin on the Isle of Skye.

At the end of the road is Mallaig (pop. 900), a small but busy village with shops, hotels and basic services, and a seasonal Tourist Information Centre. The small museum located at the railway station is worth a visit and is a good place to buy local pamphlets. There is a car ferry from Mallaig to Armadale, on the Isle of Skye, and ferry connections from Mallaig to the islands of Rum, Eigg, Muck and Canna.

These districts of the West Highlands are remote, difficult to access and lacking in some of the facilities and services modern tourists take for granted. But traditional Highland hospitality, and the magnificence of the landscape, more than compensate. It is not a place to hurry, so leave plenty of time to negotiate the twisting single-track roads. It is a place to relax in, and to enjoy the natural environment, and the scenic vistas.

At the head of Loch Linnhe, where the sea meets the mountains, lies the town of Fort William, busy, bustling with tourists and climbers, with a full range of shops and services. The town is separated from the foreshore by a rare stretch of Highland dual-carriageway, carrying traffic away from the pedestrian mall of the town centre. The population of the Fort William area, including the adjacent settlements of Caol and Corpach, now exceeds 10,000.

Fort William takes its name from the male half of the joint monarchs William and Mary. General Monk built the first fort there in 1654 to replace the fort at the mouth of the Lochy river, one mile (1.6 km) to the north. Confusingly, he took the name of the old fort with him to the new site, and called it Inverlochy. It was renamed Fort William in 1690. Even more confusingly, at the end of the seventeenth century the fishing village at the head of Loch Linnhe was called Gordonsburgh, after its proprietor.

There is a busy Tourist Information Centre in the middle of the modern town where accommodation

Lochaber & Glencoe

BEN NEVIS AND LOCH EIL
'The Ben' is Britain's highest mountain at 4409 ft (1344 m) and is climbed by many thousands of visitors every year.

The district of Lochaber lies around the head of the Firth of Lorn, a great gash of sea loch cutting into the heartland of Scotland. Angled from south-east to north-west, it is a continuation of the Great Glen, the great rift valley that nearly cuts the Highlands in two, and which for thousands of years has been a communications route through the fortress of mountains which sheltered the Caledonians and other tribal peoples.

30

can be booked and where information is available on the many attractions and places of interest in the Lochaber area. The West Highland Museum in Fort William gives interesting historical background, from prehistory right up to present day aluminium processing at Alcan's two smelters in the area, at Fort William and Kinlochleven. There is a reconstruction in the Museum of a typical West Highland cottage, and important Jacobite relics are on display.

Dominating Fort William, guarding the entrance to the Great Glen, is the massive bulk of Ben Nevis. As viewed from across the loch, from the Ardgour shore or from the village of Corpach at the entrance to Loch Eil, 'The Ben' looks gigantic but lumpishly climbable, luring thousands of visitors each summer up the 'tourist path'. But appearances are deceptive. The traditional view of Ben Nevis disguises the cliffs and gulleys on its northern face, the habitat of generations of British climbers cutting their climbing teeth before moving on to the more demanding (but not always more difficult) mountain challenges of the Alps and the Himalayas.

Ben Nevis is dangerous for tourists and climbers alike. Soaring to the dizzy height (for Scotland) of 4406 ft (1343 m), climbing it demands respect, proper equipment and proper planning. The climate of Ben Nevis can change quickly and dramatically, and many summer visitors have started off in sunny, warm conditions, only to be surprised by deteriorating weather. A successful climb takes a full day for most people.

The view from the summit on a clear day is well worth the effort. The panorama westwards, across a

landscape of lochs and mountains to the islands, is especially worthwhile.

Ageing or very young visitors may find the exertion too much, and an easier option is to take the short cable-car ride up to the Aonach Mor ski area just north of Fort William, on the northern flanks of Ben Nevis. From here, in winter, there is access to the ski slopes. The extensive panoramic view from the cable-car terminal and restaurant is rewarding for those who cannot attempt a more energetic excursion into the mountains.

South of the Corran Narrows the main road from Fort William passes through the villages of Onich and Ballachulish, where there is a choice of continuing south into Appin and Argyll and the town of Oban, or

BEN NEVIS can be climbed via the well-known 'tourist route', but you will miss out on the mountain's massive scale. An ascent of the northern side presents a serious challenge to even accomplished mountaineers.

branching off through Glencoe to Crianlarich, Loch Lomond and Glasgow. The mountains around Glencoe draw many visitors, especially to the ski slopes in winter, but the massacre of the MacDonalds of Glencoe by Government troops under the leadership of Campbell of Glen Lyon in the cold winter of 1692 tempers any enjoyment of the dramatic scenery.

Glencoe was a small-scale massacre even by the standards of the time – 38 men, women and children were slaughtered in cold blood by government troops under the command of Captain Robert Campbell of Glenlyon. Some 200 others escaped; some of them died in blizzards in the surrounding hills. The massacre took place in the early hours of 13 February 1692, in the depths of a bitterly cold winter. There was nothing unusual about clan feuding, even on the brink of the eighteenth century, but what horrified the public at large, even then, was the way in which the full force of the state was brought to bear on defenceless civilians, using a legal technicality as justification.

Glenlyon's company of about 60 officers and men, and a second company under the command of Capt. Thomas Drummond, were billeted throughout the glen for 13 days, accepting hospitality from their MacDonald hosts. Highlanders take hospitality seriously, and give it unstintingly, so when the soldiers rose at five o'clock on a cold February morning and set about their work it was the abuse of the Highland hospitality as much as the brutality of the killing which besmirched the name of Campbell.

Even before this, the MacDonalds had cause to hate the Campbells, who had usurped the power previously

GLENCOE. One of the Three Sisters above the Pass of Glencoe.

exercised by the Lords of the Isles. After the massacre of Glencoe, enmity between the two most powerful Highland clans attained an intensity which reaches down to the present day. Ultimate responsibility lay with the King, William III, and his Scottish ministers.

The King's personal orders authorising the massacre, written on 16 January 1692, referred specifically to the MacDonalds of Glencoe: 'it will be a proper vindication of the publick justice to extirpate that sect of thieves'.

The brutalities of 1692 did not quench the fighting spirit of the MacDonalds of Glencoe. In 1715 the younger son of the next MacIan led 100 Glencoe men at the battle of Sheriffmuir, while in 1745 the clan chief himself fought with 150 followers at the battle of Culloden.

For anybody familiar with this sad story, the majestic buttresses of the Glencoe mountains seem to brood over MacIan of Glencoe, Alasdair MacDonald, and his clansmen.

Glencoe meets the seacoast of Loch Leven near the narrows connecting Ballachulish to Onich. The

Ballachulish Bridge opened in the 1970s, replacing an earlier car ferry famous for its summer queues. Ballachulish was the centre of an important slate industry from the seventeenth century until the last quarries closed in the 1950s. An alternative to whizzing over the new bridge en route to Glencoe or Oban is the 23 miles (37 km) of winding road around Loch Leven. At the head of the loch is Kinlochleven, straddling the boundary of the old counties of Inverness-shire and Argyll. The aluminium factory,

GAIRICH overlooks Loch Quoich, at the head of Glen Garry. Its name means roaring. Glen Kingie lies hidden behind the mountain to the south.

33

*LOCH HOURN & KNOYDART
Looking along Loch Hourn and into Barrisdale Bay to Knoydart, an area devastated by the Clearances. One of the more remote and inaccessible parts of the Highlands, it is a challenging area for hill-walkers.*

opened in 1908 using water power from the Blackwater reservoir, provides employment and, indeed, the very reason for this village's existence.

At the head of Loch Linnhe, just to the west of Fort William, the Caledonian Canal reaches the sea at Corpach, descending the eight locks of 'Neptune's Staircase'. Most of the traffic using the canal these days is recreational, though it is still important for the fishing fleet. Linking the three lochs of the Great Glen, Loch Lochy, Loch Oich and Loch Ness, the canal itself amounts to 22 miles (35.4 km) out of the total 60 miles (96.5 km) of the Great Glen from Fort William to Inverness.

North of Fort William, just outside the village of

Spean Bridge, is the Commando Memorial, designed by Scott Sutherland in 1952. This area was used for training during the Second World War (1939-45). The view from the memorial over the Ben Nevis massif is impressive. Roy Bridge, east of Spean Bridge, gives access to Glen Roy, where the 'Parallel Roads' on the mountainside caused puzzlement for centuries until they were finally interpreted as the fluctuating shoreline marks of a glacial lake.

On the western fringes of Lochaber is the remote district of Knoydart, a mountain wilderness only accessible by boat from Mallaig. This is also the ferry port for the Small Isles, the four little islands of Rum, Eigg, Muck and Canna. If small is beautiful, then this

is the place to be. Although the populations of these communities are tiny, the islands are viable working units – just.

Eigg is only 6.5 by 4 miles (10.5 by 6.4 km) in size, but is easily recognised by the distinctive shape of An Sgurr, the ridge of columnar pitchstone identifiable from far and wide. There is a superb view from the summit. This is home to a colony of Manx shearwater, which burrow into the ground for nesting and put the fear of Thor into early Norse settlers who took their strange wailing sounds, at night, to come from underground trolls.

In 1577 practically the entire population of Eigg was suffocated in a cave by Macleods from Skye. The atrocity took place in winter; the hideout was given away by footprints in the snow. The Macleods piled brushwood at the entrance to the cave and set fire to it, killing about 395 men, women and children.

Eigg has been in the headlines for happier reasons in recent times, as the local people banded together to purchase their island estate from their controversial laird. It is now owned and administered by the Isle of

Eigg Trust.

Rum is administered by Scottish Natural Heritage as a place to study the natural history of an island; visitors can stay in luxury at Kinloch Castle, a late Victorian mansion, now a hotel.

Canna is owned by the National Trust for Scotland. It was made famous by its last laird, the folklorist and Gaelic scholar, John Lorne Campbell. Muck is the tiniest of the Small Isles, home to less than 30 people.

RUM
Looking across to the island of Rum, one of the four Small Isles from a pristine beach near Arisaig. The three other Small Isles are Eigg, Muck and Canna.

35

Skye & Lochalsh

The Misty Isle of Skye (in Gaelic, *An t-Eilean Sgitheanach*) is the largest of the Inner Hebrides. Skye is deceptively big: 535 sq miles (1385 sq km), with a complicated topography consisting of many fingers of land separated by sea lochs penetrating far inland, forming 350 miles (563 km) of coastline. It is easy to run up a hefty mileage during a week's motoring holiday in Skye: the island is 50 miles (80 km) long and from 7 to 25 miles (11 to 40 km) broad, with an extensive road system. On the other hand, it is just as easy to fall in love with one little corner of the island and spend all your time there, exploring its landscape and its past.

There is plenty to see and do in Skye, and many visitors return again and again, never tiring of its constantly changing landscapes as weather patterns reveal nuances of light and shade that cause even the locals to pause and be grateful that they live in such an awesomely beautiful place. It can be harsh and unforgiving too, and not just in winter – anybody planning excursions in the hills and mountains should be well prepared, and aware that they are in some of the most challenging and demanding wilderness in Europe.

History is all around, in the form of castles, prehistoric forts and ancient burial cairns. Most local people will have stories of clan battles, Danish princesses and folk heroes, because Skye has been a battleground for thousands of years, a place where different peoples mixed and often clashed, before settling down in harmony. To explore Skye thoroughly is the task of a lifetime, and you will never run out of surprises. Skye is an ideal holiday destination for many different kinds of people. If you are a car tourist, there are roads to most parts of the island, and if you actually enjoy driving, you will find some of the most challenging roads in Britain. If you are more energetic, you will find that Skye's reputation as a mecca for climbers and hill-walkers is well deserved. It is a mountainous island, but cyclists should not be too deterred by that, for most of the roads keep to the valley floors, or after an initial climb, traverse relatively flat moorland.

All those interested in the natural environment will find themselves fully occupied, and likely to enjoy experiences they will remember for a lifetime. The geology is spectacular. It is not necessary to have your own transport to get around as there are bus services to most townships, and these routes can often be linked up by interesting walks across country. No part of the island is more than 5 miles (8 km) from the sea, so the scenery is superb, with constantly changing combinations of mountains, moorlands and sea lochs.

Skye has a rich and varied range of archaeological and historical monuments, testimony to its long and often turbulent history. Of particular interest are the brochs of Dun Ardtreck, near Carbost, and Dun Beag, just west of Bracadale, both of which were very neatly built with square-sided facing stones. These ruins were originally stone towers up to 30 ft (9 m) high, masterpieces of Iron Age architecture, with hollow, double-skinned walls to lessen the weight and make the great height possible.

Skye is part of the heartland of Gaelic culture, with a

THE CUILLIN HILLS, Isle of Skye (opposite). Gabbro and other igneous rocks form a landscape of massive cliffs and razor-sharp peaks. Climbing here requires considerable skill and experience.

ARDTRECK
POINT AND
ORONSAY,
Isle of Skye.
The calm waters of
Loch Bracadale on the
west coast of Skye
contain many inlets
and headlands.
Among them, Ardtreck
Point and its light-
house guard the
entrance to Loch
Harport. Oronsay, in
the distance, has a
name which comes
from Old Norse
meaning ebb island.

large proportion of the population of 8500 speaking the Gaelic language in everyday life. As in other parts of the Hebrides, this culture is under threat, especially from incomers, but there is a resurrection of interest in Gaelic culture which is greatly assisted by a Gaelic college (*Sabhal Mor Ostaig*), Gaelic poetry (for example, that of the late Sorley Maclean from neighbouring Raasay), Gaelic rock music (Run Rig), a winning shinty team, and a radical local newspaper (*The West Highland Free Press*), with economic support from Highlands and Islands Enterprise and spiritual underpinning from the Sabbatarian Free Church. Museums and heritage centres, for example at Luib, Colbost, Glendale, Kilmuir, Portree and Armadale, help to interpret crofting society and island history to visitors.

The 'Skye Boat Song', beloved of generations of Scottish schoolchildren and therefore sung in the farthest corners of the English-speaking world,

commemorates the visit of Bonnie Prince Charlie to Skye. In Kilmuir burial ground is the grave of Flora MacDonald and a monument to her, the most famous lady in Skye's long history. The monument has Dr Johnson's epitaph engraved on it: 'Her name will be mentioned in history and if courage and fidelity be virtues, mentioned with honour'. It was she who helped Bonnie Prince Charlie to escape capture after the defeat at Culloden in 1746, by transporting him in a boat from her home island of North Uist, 'over the sea to Skye'. When Flora's part in the prince's escape became known, she was arrested and spent almost a year in the Tower of London. After a busy life, including some 12 years in North Carolina, she returned to her husband's house at Kingsburgh; she died in Skye in 1790, and it is said that her funeral was the largest ever witnessed in the Highlands.

Between 1840 and 1888 the native culture came

under serious threat when an estimated 30,000 islanders emigrated. The Battle of the Braes, in 1882, was a confrontation over grazing rights between local farmers and crofters in the Braes district near Portree and 50 Glasgow policemen who were imported to keep control. After a pitched battle, gunboats were sent and a force of marines landed at Uig. There was a public outcry and as a result a Royal Commission was established by Gladstone; the outcome was the Crofters Act of 1886 which provided security of tenure at a fair and controlled rent. This system, which replaced the original communal townships, remains in force today.

Travelling to Skye is easier now than at any time in the past, thanks to the new toll bridge from Kyle of Lochalsh to Kyleakin, opened in 1995, replacing the short ferry crossing. Undoubtedly it is the most revolutionary development to hit Skye for many centuries and opinion is divided as to its long-term effects. The tolls are bitterly resented by the locals, who have waged a long campaign against charges.

From Kyleakin there is a good, fast, new road to Broadford, a lively village of 900 people, with craft shops and an annual folk festival. From here a scenic road leads eventually to Elgol, from where there is a

LOCH SCAVAIG & THE CUILLIN HILLS, Isle of Skye. A classic view of the Cuillin from Elgol, looking across Loch Scavaig. The extremes of the landscape here are often matched by those of the weather.

THE QUIRAING, ISLE OF SKYE
This unusual construction of cliffs on the Trotternish peninsula looms over the crofting township of Staffin. The rock structures were formed by basalt lavas that have collapsed over the weaker underlying sedimentary rocks.

including a Tourist Information Centre. Its name (*Port an righ*, 'the King's port') derives from the visit of James V in 1540, on an expedition to quell insurrections among the rebellious population of the Western Isles. In this aim he was notably successful.

From Portree the road system diverges in all directions: to the north is the Trotternish peninsula, which has a road right round its coastline, and a small connecting road over the moor from Uig to Staffin. Right at the north of Trotternish is Duntulm Castle, a picturesque ruin, not to be missed. There are views from here across the Minch to the Outer Hebrides.

To the south-west of Portree is Minginish, reached either by a

fine view, in good weather, of the Cuillin ridge. Just before Broadford another road turns south to the Sleat peninsula, winding its way down past Sabhal Mor Ostaig to the ferry pier at Armadale, connecting with the mainland at Mallaig.

From Broadford the main road to Portree follows the coast to the head of Loch Ainort and then climbs steeply beneath Lord MacDonald's Forest and Glamaig to Loch Sligachan, then through Glen Varragill to Portree. There are fantastic views of the sea lochs and offshore islands. Portree, with a population of over 1000, is the main town, with all the usual services,

moorland road to Loch Harport or by a road turning off through Glen Drynoch at Sligachan. Climbers, hillwalkers, hostellers and serious mountaineering types head to Glen Brittle in Minginish, while thirsty car tourists may be tempted beyond Carbost to Talisker, and the distillery there.

In the north-west part of the island there are two more peninsulas, Duirinish and Waternish (or Vatternish). The peninsulas are separated by Loch Dunvegan, at the head of which is the world-famous MacLeod stronghold, Dunvegan Castle, an ancient fortress still lived in by the chief of Clan MacLeod.

On the western edge of Duirinish is Neist Point, with its lighthouse (now automated). From the road above the headland there are panoramic and dramatic views of the sea cliffs and the far-off Outer Hebrides across the Minch.

Off the eastern coast of Skye is the island of Raasay, reached by car ferry from Sconser. In 1773 James Boswell, while escorting Dr Samuel Johnson on a tour of the Hebrides, 'danced a Highland dance' on the summit of Dun Caan, the highest hill. The current population is about 180. Raasay House, home of the MacLeods of Raasay, was burned by Government troops in 1746, after Culloden. The rebuilt house was run as a hotel from 1937 to 1960, after which it became a dilapidated ruin. It is now used as the base for an excellent outdoor centre and adventure school.

On the east side of the island is Brochel Castle, built by the MacLeods of Lewis in the fifteenth century. It is built on volcanic rock, its only entrance being from the east, along a steep, narrow ridge. This ruin is in a dangerous state, and should not be approached too closely. The 2 miles (3.2 km) of road joining Brochel to Arnish are known as 'Calum's Road' and are the work of one man, Calum MacLeod, who died in 1988 soon after building it single-handedly after the local council had turned down his requests for proper access to his home. It took him between 10 and 15 years, using just a pick, a shovel, a wheel-barrow, and a manual

*PORTREE
The administrative capital of Skye.*

DUNVEGAN CASTLE, stronghold of the MacLeod Clan.

Raasay is the native island of the Gaelic poet Sorley Maclean, who died in 1996. Writing in Gaelic and English, his work was highly regarded internationally, and he was often described as Britain's greatest living poet. His brother Calum was the author of *The Highlands*, an evocative and perceptive work. Sorley Maclean was born in 1911 in the township of Osgaig, near which a cairn has been built in his honour. In subject matter his poems range from the horrors of war in the North African desert to the landscapes and woods of Skye and Raasay. His poem *Hallaig* was

THE SKYE BRIDGE, opened in 1995, sweeps across the narrow stretch of water separating Skye and the mainland. The village of Kyle of Lochalsh lies on the left, with Kyleakin on Skye opposite.

of road-making which cost him 3s (15p). Raasay Community Council decided to honour his achievement with a cairn, which was unveiled in 1990, with a suitable plaque in Gaelic and English.

Raasay has an iron-ore mine which was operated by German prisoners of war during World War I. The processing plant can still be seen, and also the course of a quarry railway, although most of the machinery was removed for scrap in the 1920s. It is possible to view the entrances to the quarry tunnels, although going inside the old mines is not recommended.

described in *The Scotsman* as a 'passionate lament for a lost society which lives on only in the poet's mind, a poem in which a whole culture gathers itself for a definitive statement'. The walk from the road end at North Fearns along the old track to the Hallaig Woods, then back over Dun Caan to Raasay House, is a fine half-day excursion. Raasay is a bastion of the Free Church with its strongly held Sabbatarian beliefs, so there is no Sunday ferry service to the island.

After this whirlwind tour of Skye and Raasay, spare a thought for the few hundred residents of the adjacent

mainland district of Lochalsh. The brochs at Glenelg are the best-preserved on the Scottish mainland, and give an excellent idea of how these Iron Age stone towers were constructed. A small, seasonal car ferry links Glenelg with Kylerhea, on Skye.

On Loch Duich is the popular twentieth-century reconstruction of Eilean Donan Castle, at Dornie, associated with the Macrae clan. Originally fortified in the thirteenth century, the medieval castle was comprehensively destroyed by a British naval bombardment in 1719, after the Battle of Glenshiel, in which a small force of Jacobites supported by 300 Spanish soldiers were comprehensively defeated by a Hanoverian army. Eilean Donan is possibly one of the most easily recognised images of a Scottish castle, having been restored in the 1930s by Colonel Macrae-Gilstrap to the designs of George Mackie Watson.

Eilean Donan castle is open to the public; the island is now linked to the mainland by a causeway.

At the head of Loch Duich are the Five Sisters of Kintail, a ridge comprising some of the grandest mountain scenery in Scotland. It continues eastwards over four more mountains, ending not far from the Cluanie Inn. Access to these mountains from the main road is easy, but since the whole ridge is 9.3 miles (15 km) long and includes six Munros (mountains over 3000 ft/914 m), it is not advisable to attempt a traverse of the whole ridge in one day. An expedition taking in the Five Sisters, on the other hand, makes an excellent one-day expedition.

The western slopes of Sgurr Fhuaran, the highest of the Five Sisters, are reputedly the longest continuous grass slope in the Highlands, dropping steeply almost to the roadside in Glen Shiel, far below.

EILEAN DONAN CASTLE and Loch Duich. The original medieval castle, once an ancient Macrae stonghold, was destroyed by a British naval bombardment in the eighteenth century. The present castle was rebuilt from the ruins in the 1930s.

Wester Ross & Ullapool

LIATHACH, TORRIDON, WESTER ROSS
The powerful ramparts of 'The Grey One' rise above Torridon village, in one of the most dramatic mountain landscapes of the Highlands.

The west coast of the Highlands north of Kyle of Lochalsh is a land of sculpted mountain peaks, sinuous sea lochs winding their way deep into the coastal landscape, wonderful sunsets, crofting townships, sandy beaches and dramatic cliff scenery. The road system, often single-track, has all sorts of interesting twists and turns to explore, though in the busy summer months time and patience are needed to negotiate some stretches. The district name for the west side of the old amalgamated county of Ross and Cromarty is Wester Ross, to distinguish it from Easter Ross on the eastern side of the country north of Dingwall, facing the North Sea. The main town of Wester Ross is Ullapool, ferry gateway to Stornoway and the Western Isles.

Driving west from Dingwall along the main cross-country route to Ullapool, under the lumpish mass of Ben Wyvis, the road passes through the spa town of Strathpeffer, where wealthy southern visitors once came annually to take the waters and get their names listed in the local newspaper. In recent years some of the Victorian buildings have been restored and renovated, and a Museum of Childhood opened.

At Garve the road divides, with one branch heading westwards to Loch Maree, Torridon and Applecross, and the other winding northwards to Ullapool. The mountains of Torridon dominate this landscape: Old Red Sandstone carved into spectacular shapes by glaciers, capped with hard, resistant quartzite. In the final minutes of a west-coast sunset, the red bands of sandstone and the white quartzite summits gleam in vibrant colours. Beinn Eighe and Liathach are the most dramatic peaks, with Beinn Alligin and Beinn Dearg to the west and north. The Torridon estate has been run by the National Trust for Scotland since 1967; with the addition of an area to the west of the main estate in 1968 it now controls over 16,000 acres (6475 ha) of unsurpassed

mountain scenery between Loch Torridon to the south and Loch Maree to the north.

The three great mountains of Torridon have names familiar to Munro-baggers and hill-walkers everywhere: Beinn Alligin, Ben Eighe and, highest of all, Liathach. The red Torridonian sandstone which makes up the bulk of Liathach and Ben Eighe is reckoned as being 750 million years old, while the white quartzite of their summit ridges is a mere 600 million years of age. Geologists, as well as climbers and hill-walkers, make their way to the mountain fortresses of Torridon in their pursuit of a wilderness experience unrivalled anywhere else in Scotland.

Access to these mountains is straightforward, but for this reason they often prove more lethal than more remote peaks, and deserve respect at any season of the year, but especially in winter.

Farther west is the Applecross peninsula, facing the islands of Raasay and Skye. A new road runs round the coast connecting Shieldaig to Applecross, but it would be a shame to visit this ancient village, where St Maelrubha founded an early Christian monastery in the seventh century, without experiencing the older road over the hill from Kishorn, through the Bealach na Ba, 'the pass of the cattle'. This road rises from sea-level to a height of 2054 ft (626 km) within 6 miles (9.7 km), with a maximum gradient of 1 in 4 (25%). Its hairpin bends and twists and turns approaching the top of the pass are an

TORRIDON
The red Torridonian sandstone of the region dates from about 750 million years ago.

*LOCH DROMA,
WESTER ROSS
at dusk.*

*THE SUMMER
ISLES from Rhue
near Ullapool.*

exciting and unforgettable driving experience, certainly not for the faint-hearted. The final viewpoint at the top gives amazing views across to the islands of Raasay and Skye.

The presence of St Maelrubha's monastery at Applecross, founded in AD 673, shows that this was not always a quiet and isolated little village on an almost inaccessible peninsula. St Maelrubha was one of the most important, and most influential of the early Christian saints with dedications in the Hebrides as far south as Islay (Kilarrow). Nothing now remains of St Maelrubha's monastery, though the current church is probably built on its site.

The alpine Applecross road reaches the coast at Kishorn, with the remains of an oil-rig construction yard; from here the road winds around Loch Carron to Stromeferry and Plockton, a prettily whitewashed village which vies with Eilean Donan and Loch Maree for its place on Scottish calendars. Slioch, the photogenic mountain on the east side of Loch Maree, is best viewed from the road along the west side of the loch, leading to Gairloch.

Plockton used to be a sleepy fishing and crofting village, but is one of many West Highland villages which has adapted to changing times. In summer it is clogged with visitors eager to enjoy its prettiness and its beautiful setting.

From Plockton it is only a short drive to Kyle of

Lochalsh and the Skye Bridge, with access to the Isle of Skye to the west and to Loch Duich, Kintail and Glen Shiel to the east, from where it is possible to complete a most interesting circuit by continuing through Glen Moriston to Loch Ness and Inverness.

Gairloch is a village and fishing port, with a fine little heritage museum, famous for the views and coastal scenery around Loch Gairloch. The sandy shores provide good bathing and fishing. The islands in the beautiful sea loch, and the views to the south and south-west, combine to give this small village one of the loveliest settings in the Scottish Highlands.

Away to the south-west, across the Inner Sound, there are distant views of the Cuillin Hills in the southern part of the island of Skye. Southwards, the view is of the Flowerdale Forest and Shieldaig Forest peaks, with beyond them Beinn Alligin and the mountains of Torridon.

From Gairloch a narrow but highly scenic road runs north towards Melvaig, beyond which is the lonely Rudha Reidh, with a lighthouse. South of

Gairloch another spur of road passes through the crofting townships of Badachro, Opinan and South Erradale.

Just 5 miles (8 km) to the east of Gairloch is Poolewe, where Inverewe Gardens, a National Trust for Scotland property, was created out of almost nothing by Osgood Mackenzie when he took over the house in 1862. Over the years he created an unexpected corner of horticultural paradise in the soft, mild, west coast climate, with trees and shrubs from all over the

PLOCKTON at the entrance to Loch Carron, with the Applecross peninsula behind. Once a busy fishing and crofting village, Plockton is now a popular stop for visitors.

47

ULLAPOOL,
Loch Broom,
looking towards Beinn
Ghobhlach. Ullapool
was founded in the
eighteenth century as
a port for herring
fishing. Today it is the
largest village in
Wester Ross and a
ferry terminal for the
Western Isles.

important centre of naval operations during the war and was used for assembling convoys. Aultbea became a major NATO supply base.

Ullapool is the largest village in Wester Ross, with a population of just over 1000. It is situated on a promontory jutting out into Loch Broom, a sea loch. Ullapool was founded by the British Fisheries Society in 1788 as one of a series of projects intended to exploit the herring fishery, but by 1830 it was clear that herring stocks were in decline and the village never fulfilled its early promise. There is a small museum. Today, tourism, and the Ullapool–Stornoway ferry service, form the core of the local economy, with seasonal fishing on a small scale. From time to time, depending on circumstances well outside local control, Loch Broom fills up with Russian and Eastern European factory ships, known as 'klondykers', which buy up catches from the local fishing fleet and for a few weeks each year turn Ullapool into a cosmopolitan enclave.

Despite its isolation, Ullapool has acquired something of a reputation as a centre of cultural and literary pursuits, due in large part to the innovative

world. By his death in 1922 there were over 2500 species. The waters of the Gulf Stream, coupled with loving care and great gardening skills, are responsible for what is now one of the major tourist attractions in the north of Scotland.

North of Poolewe, a road winds round the coast to Ullapool, passing Loch Ewe and Aultbea, Gruinard Bay, and Little Loch Broom. Gruinard Island was used during the Second World War for experiments with anthrax bombs, and has only recently been de-contaminated and declared safe. Loch Ewe was an and creative interest of the owners of The Ceilidh Place, a local hostelry and restaurant. During the long northern winters, poetry readings and art exhibitions enliven the local scene.

Across Loch Broom, at Altnaharrie, is one of Scotland's most famous restaurants. Also on the isolated west shore of Loch Broom, at Rhiroy, an Iron Age broch is a reminder of many centuries of cultural excellence.

The ferry journey across the Minch to Stornoway takes a little over two-and-a-half hours in good weather. A fast, modern car ferry operated by Caledonian MacBrayne has improved reliability on this essential link between the mainland and the Western Isles. Other services operate from Uig, on the island of Skye, to Tarbert in Harris and to Lochmaddy in North Uist, while the southern sector of the Outer Hebrides is served from Oban, in Argyll, from where Calmac ferries sail to Barra and South Uist.

North of Ullapool, on the fringes of the spectacular mountains of Sutherland, a road turns west for Achiltibuie, an isolated part of Wester Ross famous for the view of the Summer Isles, a scatter of islands at

the entrance to Loch Broom. Sir Frank Fraser Darling, Scotland's most famous naturalist and ecologist, farmed Tanera Mor during the years of the Second World War. This experience, chronicled in his book *Island Farm*, of successfully cultivating land which was once home to over one hundred people, but by the 1930s was abandoned and deserted, gave him the confidence and impetus to undertake his *West Highland Survey*, perhaps the most important piece of research in the Highlands into what he described as 'human ecology'.

INVERPOLLY
Looking westwards from Knochan across Inverpolly National Nature Reserve to the sandstone peak of Stac Pollaidh in the distance.

The Black Isle & Easter Ross

CROMARTY, on the Black Isle, has retained much of its fine eighteenth-century architecture.

Confusingly, the Black Isle is not an island, and it is not black. It is a peninsula jutting out into the North Sea at the 'corner' of the Moray Firth, bounded on its north side by the Cromarty Firth and on the south side by the Beauly Firth, joined to the mainland at the villages of Beauly and Muir of Ord. Once a rather isolated and traditional part of the Highlands, the new Kessock Bridge carrying the A9 trunk road north from Inverness across the Beauly Firth has rendered its southern shores a suburb of the Highland capital and brought the whole of the Black Isle within commuting distance.

Its name is thought to derive from its appearance from out at sea, from where the peaty Milbuie ridge gave a dark appearance to the higher ground of the peninsula, before most of the peat was cut for fuel by the middle of the nineteenth century for the fires of Fortrose, Rosemarkie and Cromarty, the principal villages.

The main town is Cromarty, at the point of the peninsula, looking across to the Hill of Nigg and the oil construction yard nearby. The two headlands guarding the entrance to the Cromarty Firth are known as the 'Sutors of Cromarty'. Until the nineteenth century Cromarty and Inverness vied for the honour of the best port and anchorage in the area, but where Inverness prospered, Cromarty lapsed. One result of this is that whereas in Inverness only a handful of older buildings survive, in Cromarty there

is a largely unaltered eighteenth-century town, now a conservation area.

There are some seventeenth-century buildings, one of which is owned by the National Trust for Scotland, for it is the birthplace of Hugh Miller (1802-56), the Cromarty stone mason who taught himself geology and journalism and was one of the best known personalities of nineteenth-century Scotland. He shot himself on Christmas Eve 1856, unable to reconcile his scientific observation with the creation story of the Book of Genesis. Other early geologists insisted, correctly, on the great age of the earth's rocks, while Miller strove to reconcile the new knowledge with the Bible, but eventually was no longer able to sustain his position. He was a complex man, with a dark and detached personality. The Museum in his cottage contains much interesting material.

The Cromarty Courthouse, finished in 1783, is a handsome Georgian building, now converted for use as the town's museum and heritage centre, with animated models re-creating a trial. Sir Thomas Urquhart (1611-60), writer and professional eccentric, was the laird of Cromarty. He attempted to invent a universal language which reads as well backwards as forwards, offered a new theory of trigonometry, was imprisoned by Cromwell for being too ardent a royalist, and supposedly died of an uncontrollable fit of laughter on hearing of the Restoration of Charles II.

Fortrose is another ancient town, with a ruined cathedral dating from the middle of the thirteenth century. One of the Lords of the Isles is buried there, by virtue of his joint title of Earl of Ross. Coinneach Odhar, 'the Brahan Seer', was supposedly burnt in a barrel of tar on Chanonry Point, where an attractive lighthouse looks across the narrows to Fort George.

CHANONRY LIGHTHOUSE, near Fortrose. This promontory, opposite Fort George, is a popular place for viewing bottlenose dolphins in the Moray Firth.

As the Millennium approaches, there is a revival of interest in his 'prophesies', written up and published by Alexander Mackenzie in 1877. Modern scholars and historians have difficulty reconciling the many tales attributed to the Brahan Seer with the historical record.

Adjoining Fortrose is the little village of Rosemarkie. The 'rose' element in both names derives from the 'ross' or promontory of Chanonry Point. Rosemarkie has the little Groam House Museum, specialising in the history of the mysterious Picts. There is a collection of carved Pictish stones, as well as the important Rosemarkie cross, an intricately carved example of Pictish art.

At the neck of the Black Isle is the village of Beauly, with a ruined priory, founded in 1230 by French Valliscaulian monks. The name 'Beauly' derives from the French 'beau lieu', beautiful place. This area is associated with the Frasers of Lovat, whose ancestral home at Beaufort Castle nearby, and most of their estates, had to be sold in the 1990s to pay off massive debts.

Near the head of the Cromarty Firth is the ancient town of Dingwall, the county town of Ross and Cromarty, now rather overshadowed by its more prosperous neighbour across the Kessock Bridge, only 20 minutes away. With a population of 5000, Dingwall has a long history, having been created a Royal Burgh in 1226. There was an important castle, of which only slight traces remain. The Tolbooth dates from 1730 and contains a small museum. Tulloch Castle, formerly the seat of the Davidsons, is now a hotel. Overlooking the town is a prominent tower crowning the town's

cemetery, commemorating General Sir Hector MacDonald, a local crofter's son who through military prowess gained the title of 'Fighting Mac'. He served in Afghanistan, Egypt and the Sudan, covering himself with glory. He shot himself in a Paris hotel room in 1903, following allegations about his private life. Local people refused to entertain any suggestion of infamy and rather overcompensated in their memorial.

Along the shores of the Cromarty Firth are the villages of Evanton, Alness and Invergordon, where there was an important naval base. It was originally Inverbreakie, but was renamed when acquired and rebuilt by Sir William Gordon of Embo in the eighteenth century. A new causeway across the Cromarty Firth carrying the A9 trunk road has brought these towns closer to Inverness. The population grew in the 1970s due to the growth of oil rig construction yards in the area, and associated engineering enterprises, and the yard at Nigg survives, just.

Further north is the ancient royal burgh of Tain, associated with St Duthac. It was an important pilgrimage centre in the Middle Ages. A small museum beside the church interprets the history of the town. To the east of Tain another peninsula juts out into the north sea, ending at Tarbat Ness. The village of Portmahomack is unusual in being an east-coast town which faces west, with good views of Ben Wyvis and the mountains of Sutherland. The so-called 'Seaboard Villages' of Hilton of Cadboll, Balintore and Shandwick, on the east coast of the peninsula, are small traditional fishing villages giving a glimpse of a former way of life. At Shandwick an important Pictish stone has recently been conserved and a protective

shelter erected around it.

Returning to the 'neck' of the Black Isle, a road runs south-west through the district of The Aird, through Kilmorack, overlooking the former Lovat seat of Beaufort Castle, no longer owned by the Flemish Fraser family who first settled in this area in the early Middle Ages. The road continues past the lands of Aigas, where the charlatan Sobieski Stuart brothers peddled their fakery – they claimed to be descendants of Bonnie Prince Charlie and produced a book of bogus history, lavishly illustrated, under the title

Vestiarium Scoticum, and a fake tartan.

Continuing up Strathglass, the road eventually reaches the inland crossroads of Cannich, from where some of the most beautiful glens in the Highlands branch off in all directions. From here it is possible to head east into Glen Urquhart, rejoining Loch Ness at Drumnadrochit, but those travellers seeking the ultimate in Highland landscape will continue inland to Glen Affric, where the ancient Caledonian forest of Scots pines is regenerating under the protection of environmental agencies.

THE DORNOCH FIRTH, the border between Easter Ross and Sutherland. Far off to the west are the mountains of Inverpolly and Assynt.

Sutherland

SUILVEN,
SUTHERLAND
*Often likened to a
sugar loaf, Suilven's
quartzite-capped peak
exerts its presence on
the landscape of the
north-west.*

The old county of Sutherland was the most sparsely populated in Scotland, and today this part of Highland Council's territory has just over 13,000 people, of whom 8500 live on the east side of the county, around the Dornoch Firth and in the string of towns facing the North Sea: Dornoch, Golspie, Brora, and Helmsdale. The rest live in scattered crofting communities and small villages. The two main settlements on the Atlantic coast of Sutherland,

Lochinver and Kinlochbervie, are important fishing ports. There are vast areas of mountain and moorland, with single-track roads through the main valleys and along the coastlands. The north-west corner of the county is Cape Wrath.

Sutherland encompasses the whole of the north of Scotland north of the Dornoch Firth on the east and Ullapool on the west, except for the small county of Caithness occupying a triangle in the north-east corner of Scotland. On the east coast, access has been greatly improved by the new causeway and bridge across the entrance of the Dornoch Firth, bringing the ancient burghs of Tain and Dornoch closer together. Historically this was the boundary between the lands occupied by the Norse and the rest of Scotland: north of the Dornoch Firth the great density of Norse place-names is a permanent reminder of their influence.

Dornoch was the county town of Sutherland, and is still an important administrative centre. The Bishop's Palace, a sixteenth-century fortified tower now a hotel, and the thirteenth-century cathedral are just two of the historic and architecturally interesting buildings in this attractive town. The cathedral contains tombs and memorials to the infamous Sutherland family responsible for some of the worst excesses of the Highland Clearances. Andrew Carnegie lived at nearby Skibo Castle, a sprawling mansion now a luxury hotel. The championship links golf course at Dornoch is a major visitor attraction. The nearby village of Embo, on the coast north of Dornoch, is of note for being the last enclave of east coast Sutherland Gaelic, a linguistic pocket of the ancient language once spoken by the entire population in these parts.

Dunrobin Castle, at Golspie, further up the coast, is the seat of the Earls of Sutherland, and is open to the public. The core of the present building is a thirteenth-century stronghold, though later extensions and additions have transformed the spartan original into a fairy tale château which would seem less out of place on the Loire. Throughout the nineteenth century, and well into the twentieth, Dunrobin entertained a glittering array of interesting and titled visitors. Golspie is a company town, an estate village which owes its existence to Dunrobin. On a hilltop overlooking the town is a notorious statue commemorating the first Duke of Sutherland; George Granville Leveson-Gower (1758-1833), Marquess of Stafford after 1803, and his wife Elizabeth, Countess of Sutherland in her own right, with their agents and servants, are among the most hated individuals in the Highlands. The debate continues as to whether the statue on Beinn a' Bhragaidh should be retained as a symbol of ruthless repression and cultural genocide, or demolished as an obscene reminder of a sad period in Highland history. The real monuments to the Highland Clearances are the empty glens and roofless ruins scattered

DUNROBIN CASTLE, near Golspie, historic home of the Earls of Sutherland.

INVERNAVER
at Torrisdale Bay,
Sutherland.

OLDSHOREMORE
BEACH
in the far north-west.

throughout the whole of the Highlands and Islands.

Brora has lost two major industries in recent years: its coal mine, a victim of economic forces, and the military communications centre, closed as part of the 'peace dividend' at the end of the Cold War. Right on the northern edge of the county of Sutherland, bordering on Caithness, the village of Helmsdale has the award-winning Timespan heritage centre, where the story of the Clearances is interpreted.

The river which reaches the sea at Helmsdale is one of the great salmon fishing rivers of the Highlands. It flows through the Strath of Kildonan, where the population was reduced from 1574 in 1811 to a mere 257 by 1831, in another of the Sutherland Clearances instigated by the Countess of Sutherland. Many of the tenants evicted from Kildonan found their way across the Atlantic, but most were resettled in the coastal villages of Caithness. Ironically, later in the nineteenth century Kildonan was the centre of a small-scale gold rush, after gold was found in the Helmsdale River.

Inland from the Dornoch Firth, the village of Lairg, in the only landlocked parish in Sutherland, is renowned as a centre for cattle and sheep sales. To the north of the village is Loch Shin, now part of a large hydro-electric scheme. A single-track road continues along Loch Shin, eventually reaching the west coast at Laxford Bridge. Alternatively, another road runs due north from Lairg, passing through Altnaharra before

reaching Loch Loyal and the village of Tongue, on the north coast.

On the west side of Sutherland, on the county's Atlantic coast, the landscape is dominated by the sugar-loaf mountains of Assynt: Canisp, Suilven, Stac Pollaidh, Quinag and Ben More Assynt. The very names conjure up an image of these sculpted buttresses of Torridonian sandstone on a granite base, mountainous pillars soaring out of the surrounding moors and lochans.

The geological landscape of north-west Sutherland is of great complexity, and of great interest to students.

From Lochinver all the way north to Cape Wrath and Durness there is a coastal strip of Lewisian Gneiss, 10 miles (16 km) wide, with granite and Torridonian patches north of Scourie. But in Assynt, between Lochinver and Scourie, the landscape is almost entirely of Gneiss, a situation found nowhere else on the mainland of Scotland.

This ancient rock – the oldest in Europe – is also found in the Hebrides (especially on the Isle of Lewis, from where it takes its name), and across the Atlantic in Greenland and Newfoundland, showing that at one time there was an enormous continental landmass

KYLESKU BRIDGE
replaced the Strome Ferry in north-west Sutherland. An award-winning combination of modern concrete and ancient rock.

57

WHITEN HEAD, from the beach at Ceannabeinne, near Durness. Sutherland's northern coastline is an area of unspoiled sandy beaches and rugged cliffs.

BEN LOYAL AND THE KYLE OF TONGUE (opposite). Ben Loyal is one of the Highland's most northerly mountains.

Characteristics

My American friends,
who claim Scottish ancestry,
have been touring Scotland.
In ten days they visited
eleven castles. I smiled –
How American.

They said they preferred
the ruined ones. I smiled again.
How Scottish.

where the Atlantic ocean now is.

In recent years the crofters of Assynt bid successfully for the estate of which they were tenants, and have proved that native Highlanders can own their own land and run it profitably. The fishing ports of Lochinver and Kinlochbervie have had millions of pounds invested in pier and storage facilities and are crucial to the survival of the local fishing fleets. A new bridge carries the main road over the narrows at Kylestrome, where once a small car ferry plied its trade.

The poet Norman MacCaig, writing in English but of Assynt stock, has described the lands of north-west Sutherland beautifully in many of his poems. One of his more whimsical poems encapsulates one of the central issues facing the Highlands today:

Along the north coast, in Mackay country, a series of lochs aligned on a north-south axis point like fingers deep into the landscape: the Kyle of Durness, Loch Eriboll, Loch Hope, and the Kyle of Tongue. South of the village of Tongue is the photogenic Ben Loyal. Other spectacular mountains in north Sutherland are Foinaven and Arkle, neighbouring peaks dominating the village of Rhiconich. Near Durness, a craft village occupies former military buildings where a little community of talented incomers have grafted their way of life onto the local culture. The Smoo Cave, 2 miles (3.2 km) east of Durness, has been a tourist attraction since Sir Walter Scott's visit in 1814. Stalagmites and stalactites decorate this large limestone cave.

The now-deserted glen of Strathnaver is a name which is etched on Highland consciousness, for it was here, between 1814 and 1819 that the Duchess of Sutherland and her factor Patrick Sellar cleared all the tenants to make way for more profitable flocks of sheep. In 1816 Sellar stood trial in Inverness for the atrocities committed in his name, but was acquitted. There is a small museum in the former Farr parish church at Bettyhill, and an important ninth-century Pictish cross in the graveyard. Farr Secondary School educates scholars from a wide hinterland.

Caithness

The country of Caithness occupies the far north-eastern tip of the Scottish mainland, a triangle of bog and moorland bordered on the north coast by the rough waters of the Pentland Firth and on the east by the north sea. The population is about 25,000. The two main towns are Wick, the former county town, with about 8500 residents, and the slightly larger Thurso, with a population of 9000. This is a very distinctive area, in some ways more Lowland than Highland, though many of the population, especially in the east coast fishing villages, originated in Highland glens from where they were forcibly removed early in the nineteenth century, in the Sutherland Clearances. The local accent and dialect has more in common with Orkney than with the rest of the Highlands, and shows a strong Scandinavian influence, the result of hundreds of years of Norse occupation in the early Middle Ages. Even the geology is different: Caithness is flagstone country, where instead of drystone field dykes the boundaries are thin pieces of Caithness flagstone placed vertically in the ground.

All over the Highlands there are interesting archaeological sites, but two of the most interesting and best preserved are in Caithness, near the village of Lybster. The Neolithic Grey Cairns of Camster, over 5800 years old, were communal burial places, built with great community effort and great skill. There is a round cairn, its roof almost intact, with a burial chamber divided by slabs into three sections, while the adjacent horned cairn, 200 ft (61 m) long, is one of the finest in Scotland. Both have been excavated, and reconstructed in part. Also near Lybster, at Mid Clyth, are the enigmatic stone rows, probably dating from the Bronze Age, from around 1500 BC.

Standing stones and stone circles are commonplace throughout Scotland, but stone rows are unusual, and it has been suggested that they represent a kind of mathematical grid on which complex astronomical

calculations were worked out, relating to the orbit of the moon – linked to eclipse prediction. The only comparable sites are in Cornwall and Brittany, at the opposite end of a Bronze Age cultural province.

Wick has a history not quite as long, but certainly dates to Viking times, as its name means 'bay' in Norse. It was a royal burgh in the Middle Ages. Pultneytown, now considered part of Wick, except by the people who live there, gets its name from the patron of Thomas Telford, who was commissioned in the early

1800s to create a new harbour there. Wick was the herring capital of Europe in 1817, when 60,000 barrels were exported, but suffered with the decline of that fishery, and is still an unemployment blackspot. The world-renowned Caithness Glass factory is one success story in an otherwise depressed economy.

There is great rivalry between Wick and its neighbouring town Thurso, 20 miles (32 km) away. Sir John Sinclair of Ulbster (1754-1835), an agricultural reformer with a rare concern for the effects of his

THE FLOW COUNTRY of Caithness. This landscape of peat bogs and rich plant life is a National Nature Reserve, and an important breeding ground for moorland birds.

STACKS OF DUNCANSBY, CAITHNESS
The rocky coastline near Duncansby Head is a haven for seabirds such as guillemots and kittiwakes. Puffins also breed here in spring and summer.

nuclear reactor research facility at Dounreay, started in 1954. The fast-breeder reactor programme has come to an end, with resultant job losses, but the controversial decision to get involved in nuclear reprocessing has guaranteed the continued existence of this research centre, situated for safety reasons as far as possible from metropolitan London. Suspicions of a link between Dounreay and a 'leukemia cluster' in Caithness have never been proved, but doubts remain. It is now evident that the reactor was built too close to the shoreline, as coastal erosion is threatening to undermine waste storage shafts in the next few decades.

Both Wick and Thurso are connected to Inverness by a precarious rail link, periodically threatened with closure. There is an airport at Wick, and from Scrabster, on Thurso Bay, a car ferry connects with Orkney, with a seasonal service on to Shetland.

East of Thurso is Dunnet Head, the most northerly point of the Scottish mainland, a promontory with magnificent cliff scenery on which perches a lighthouse. The parish of Dunnet is memorable for one of its incumbents, the cartographer Timothy Pont, who single-handedly carried out the mapping of Scotland in manuscript between 1585 and 1595. He died without seeing his project realised, but 50 years

ideas on his tenantry was born in Thurso Castle. His lasting achievement is the *Statistical Account of Scotland*, of which he was the editor. This was a parish by parish history and description of Scotland as it was at the end of the eighteenth century, and is still used by historians as an unrivalled source of information on social conditions, population statistics, and historical information. Thurso was also the birthplace of Sir William Smith (1854-1914), the founder of the Boys' Brigade.

Thurso has blossomed in the last half of the twentieth century, mostly due to its proximity to the later the Amsterdam cartographic firm of Blaeu published his edited manuscripts in a magnificent atlas. Pont's maps, and Blaeu's revisions, are important sources in the study of Scottish local history.

East of Dunnet Head is John o'Groats, which is about 870 miles (1400 km) from Land's End, in Cornwall. Having praised Sir John Sinclair for his *Statistical Account*, we must now firmly allocate to him the blame for recounting there how the Dutchman Jan de Grot came to Caithness in the reign of James IV and built an octagonal house for his eight sons. The ferry service he operated to the Orkney island of South Ronaldsay, just over 6 miles (9.6 km) across the Pentland Firth, still exists today in modified form. Tourists can have their photographs taken at John o'Groats, in front of a signpost indicating the mileage to their home town.

Between Dunnet and John o'Groats is the Castle of Mey, formerly Barrogill Castle, for many years the property of Her Majesty Queen Elizabeth, the Queen Mother. The core of the castle dates from 1606.

Dunbeath, one of the herring fishery villages on the east coast of Caithness, was the birthplace of the novelist Neil Gunn (1891-1973), and is described in his writings, such as *The Grey Coast, Morning Tide, Highland River* and *The Silver Darlings*. His novels are all back in print, and their great importance recognised, after decades of unavailability. Neil Gunn's descriptions of Highland life are chronicled movingly and memorably in his writings, especially in *Highland River*, where the course of his native river to the sea is taken as a metaphor for his own growth and development.

JOHN O'GROATS, well-known as the most northerly inhabited place of mainland Britain.

INDEX

*Entries in **bold** indicate pictures*

First published in Great Britain in 1998 by Lomond Books, 36 West Shore Road, Granton, Edinburgh, EH5 1QD
Produced by Colin Baxter Photography Ltd

Photographs Copyright © Colin Baxter 1998
Text Copyright © Colin Baxter Photography Ltd 1998
The poem *Characteristics* on page 58 from Norman MacCaig's *Collected Poems* © Norman MacCaig 1985, published by Chatto & Windus
All rights reserved

A CIP catalogue record for this book is available from the British Library

ISBN 0 947782 77 X

Printed in Hong Kong

Front cover photograph: *BUACHAILLE ETIVE MÓR, GLENCOE* Back cover photograph: *LOCH GARTEN, STRATHSPEY*
Page 1 photograph: *LOCH TORRIDON, WESTER ROSS*